THE
BUSINESS LETTER WRITER

FOULSHAM'S "NEW" POPULAR HANDBOOKS

THE
BUSINESS LETTER WRITER

by
CHARLES R. CECIL

A MODERN GUIDE WITH MANY MODEL
EXAMPLES FOR ALL WHO WRITE,
DICTATE OR TYPE BUSINESS LETTERS

LONDON
W. FOULSHAM & CO. LTD.
NEW YORK - TORONTO - CAPE TOWN - SYDNEY

W. FOULSHAM & CO. LTD.,
Yeovil Road, Slough, Berks., England

ISBN 0-572-00169-X

Printed in Great Britain by Edwin Snell Printers
Copyright: W. Foulsham & Co. Ltd.

CONTENTS

CONTENTS

PART II

MODEL BUSINESS LETTERS

PREFACE

THIS book is not a text-book of a separate language called "business English." It does not tell the reader how to turn simple words into commercial jargon. It will show him how easy it is to avoid this common fault.

A good business letter should be short, clear and courteous. So-called business English, with its peculiar jargon, is long-winded, obscure, and pompous, and modern firms no longer use it. They are coming to realise that a simple sentence like "Thank you for your letter of 10th May" is shorter, clearer, and more courteous than "We are in receipt of your esteemed favour of the 10th inst."

Whether you deal with business correspondence in the course of your employment ; whether you run a business of your own, or whether you merely have occasional business letters to write as a private individual, this guide will be of assistance.

The book is divided into two parts. The first part tells how to write a business letter ; the second part gives examples of typical business letters. These specimen letters can be used as models, but the reader is advised first to study the general principles given in the earlier chapters.

PART I

HOW TO WRITE BUSINESS LETTERS

CHAPTER I

THE FRAMEWORK

WHETHER you dictate fifty letters a day to a secretary or write about a dozen letters a year by hand, you need to have some *form* in your correspondence that you can always use. The framework of a letter means everything that is typed or written except the actual contents, and if you standardize it at the start you will not have to waste any time or thought on it afterwards.

Every letter must bear the writer's address at the top. Business firms use headed writing paper, in which the name and address (and telephone number) are printed clearly across the top of the sheet. The important thing is that the type of the heading should be clear; fancy types only irritate people and often leads to replies being incorrectly addressed.

If you use plain writing paper, type or write your address in the right-hand top corner of the letter. Make sure that it is absolutely legible; and give it in full. If you live in a town with numbered postal areas, include the name of the district and town as well as the area number. For example, if your address is Park Road, Ealing, London, W.5. do not put simply Park Road, W.5." Admittedly that is enough for the post office—but remember that people make mistakes in addressing envelopes, and if someone writes " N.5 " instead of " W.5 ", the reply to your letter will certainly be delayed and may be mislaid. If you look up Park Road in an index to a map of London or any other big town you will see one of the reasons why.

Similarly, if your house has a name as well as a number, state both. The name will help the postman if someone puts the wrong number on an envelope addressed to you. Every one of us makes mistakes sometimes, and it is asking for trouble to take it for granted that no one else does. The number of the house helps the postman in sorting the letters he is delivering.

If you have a telephone, and are prepared to have your correspondent ring you up, put your exchange and number in the top left-hand corner or below your address. If you live in London or any other large town where the three-letter dialling system is used, write the first three letters of the exchange in capitals, thus : EALing.

Underneath the address—printed, typed, or written— put the date. Write it in full, including the year. Never put just the day of the week in a business letter.

If you want to give your letter a numbered reference, this should be placed on the left-hand side of the letter, about level with the last line of your address. Simply put " Ref : SQ/1234 ", or whatever it is, and underline it. If only the writer's and typist's initials are given however, this reference is typed at the foot of the letter on the left.

A few lines under this, and still on the left-hand side, comes the name and address of the person or organisation to whom you are writing. It used to be the custom to put this at the bottom of a letter, and some firms still follow this practice ; but it is dying out, and need not be regretted. A shorthand-typist, however, is well advised to query the matter tactfully before changing an employer's practice.

The name and address of your correspondent given at the top (or bottom) of your letter will be in exactly the same form as on the envelope, and it is most important that nothing should be left out.

If you are writing to a firm or other organisation, the formula is simple. If the firm's title embodies the name of an individual, you begin with the word " Messrs." thus : " Messrs. John Smith & Co. Ltd." If, however, it does not bear a personal name, leave out the " Messrs." thus : " The Hardware Wholesale Company Ltd." or " Hardware Wholesale Ltd.," as the case may be ; you just copy the registered title as given in the firm's letter-heading or in a directory. The same applies if you write to a Government or other official body. Thus : " The Ministry of National Insurance ".

However, you may not often write to a firm or official body in general. If you do not actually write to an individual by name, you will usually address your letter to a particular officer. For example, when you write to a bank you will address your letter to " The Manager ", while for a firm you may write to " The Secretary " or " The Sales Manager " or " The Advertising Manager". If you are replying to a letter from an organisation of any sort write back to the person who signed it—to his appointment if not to him personally. There is one exception to this. Some business houses print in their letter-headings the words " All communications should be addressed to the Company ". This practice is dying out, but it is not dead ; and where it still lives it should be respected. It is, however, permissible to address a letter to such a firm and, before commencing the context, insert a heading : For the attention of Mr. ———. This heading is typed or written in upper and lower case letters underlined, and should be repeated in the top or bottom left-hand corner of the envelope.

If you are writing to a person by name you must decide on the form to be used for his name in the address. First of all, be sure to put his Christian name or initials as well as his surname. " Mr. Smith " is vague and not very courteous. You may address him as " Mr. J. Smith " or " Mr. John Smith " ; but the more usual form to-day is " J. Smith, Esq." or John Smith, Esq." (You must

never put " Mr. John Smith, Esq.")   At one time " Esq."
or " Esquire " meant that the person was of a certain
social status, but this distinction has disappeared.   There
is nothing wrong with addressing a person as " Mr. John
Smith ", but in Great Britain " John Smith, Esq." is
usually considered more courteous.   No one will object
to being addressed as " Esq." instead of " Mr.", but
some men may dislike being addressed as " Mr." instead of
" Esq."   There are two exceptions.   When you do not
know the man's Christian name or initials, you can only
write " Mr. Smith ".   Some people try to get round this
by writing " —— Smith, Esq.", but that is pointless and
incorrect.   When you are writing to U.S.A. or Canada,
you may prefer to follow the practice of those countries
and use Mr., but always include the Christian name or
initial.

If the man you are writing to has any decorations or
degrees put these correct initials for them after the " Esq."
thus : " John Smith, Esq., B.A."   Address a clergyman
as " The Rev. John Smith " or " The Rev. J. Smith "—
never write " The Rev. Smith ".   There are special
forms of address to persons of title, which you can find in
reference books, such as *The Complete Letter Writer*
(Foulsham).   Decorations awarded by the Sovereign
come before academic degrees, thus : " John Brown, Esq.,
M.C., M.A." or " John Brown, Esq., O.B.E., M.A."

Underneath the name and address comes what is called
the salutation, and this may be in one of several forms.
When you are writing to a firm you have the choice of
"Sirs," "Dear Sirs", and "Gentlemen".   The first is the
least usual ; the second is the most commonly used
to-day, and is never out of place except in special kinds of
correspondence, such as that of Government Depart-
ments.   " Gentlemen " is correct when writing to a
firm whose title does not embody the name of any
individual.

If you are writing to an unnamed individual, such as
" The Manager " or " The Secretary ", you can use either

" Sir " or " Dear Sir ". Nowadays " Sir " is considered very formal indeed, although it is still used in special kinds of letters, such as those addressed to the Editor of a newspaper. " Dear Sir " is always safe.

If you are addressing your letter to a person by name, the salutation will probably be either " Dear Sir " or " Dear Mr. Smith ". If you have met him even once, or spoken to him by telephone, it is better to use " Dear Mr. Smith ". If you are replying to a letter from him, you can safely return the form of address he has used to you. " Dear Sir " is now considered rather formal and " Dear Mr. Smith " does not usually imply undue familiarity. However, it is important to consider your relationship with Mr. Smith here. If you are his customer, you can please yourself ; if he is your customer, wait for him to start addressing you by name first if you do not know him personally. It is better to be thought too formal than too familiar, and " Dear Sir " is safe for all occasions.

All that has been said above may be applied equally to correspondence with a woman, except that where " Sir " is used for a man, " Madam " is used for a woman. " Dear Sir " becomes " Dear Madam "; and " Dear Mr. Smith " becomes " Dear Mrs. Smith " or " Dear Miss Smith ". And, of course, any change from formality to familiarity should come from the woman first. The man must wait, just as he waits for the woman to hold out her hand when they are introduced. If you are not sure whether a woman is married or not, use " Miss ".

In business correspondence to-day you will often find letters beginning simply " Dear Smith " or even " Dear John ". The second form is especially common in the U.S.A. and the Dominions, where Christian names are used more readily than in Britain. (When Lord Tweedsmuir retired from the post of Governor-General of Canada he remarked that it was a fine country but " you need to know a man very well before you can call him by his surname ! ") The practice is growing in this country, and the sensible person will neither resist it nor abuse it. If someone addresses you as " Dear Smith " or " Dear John ", do not necessarily think he is being unduly familiar ; in most cases he is merely being friendly, and courtesy demands that you reply in the same form, unless he is a good deal older than yourself and you think he is entitled to more respect. Again, if you are writing to someone you know, and whom you normally call by his surname or Christian name when you speak to him, it is not always necessary to change to " Dear Mr. Smith " just because you are writing a letter. In large firms, however, business letters being filed for reference, perhaps by numerous other people, the surname may be more appropriate, particularly if you are writing to a member of the staff who is not an executive of the firm.

Do not start calling a man only by his surname or Christian name in a letter when you have never used this form of address in conversation. Do not be in a hurry to drop the " Mr." A man should never be the first to start familiarity of this sort with a woman.

Having written the salutation, you may next quote any reference number that has been used by the person or firm to whom you are writing. This should be centred on a separate line and underlined thus :

<u>Your ref : PST/3567</u>

If no reference number has been given, or if you are starting the correspondence, you may put the subject of your letter here, instead, in capital letters and underlined, thus :

<u>PACKING CASES</u>

Under this comes the main body of your letter, which will be considered in the next chapter. All that need be said here is that it should be typed or written clearly and legibly. If it is typed, a good margin should be allowed left and right, and two spaces given between sentences. The lines of a short letter should be double spaced; a longer one, single-spaced should have double spaces between paragraphs.

After the body of the letter comes what is called the subscription, which is simply the phrase used before your signature; it is centred after a double space below the last line of the letter.

There are several forms for this, but there is no need to waste time on considering them all. The one to use depends largely on the form of salutation at the beginning of the letter. If you began formally—with " Sir ", " Dear Sir ", " Dear Sirs ", " Gentlemen ", " Madam ", or " Dear Madam "—then you should end with " Yours faithfully ". If you began with a name— " Dear Mr. Smith ", " Dear Mrs. Smith " or " Dear Miss Smith "—then you will usually close with " Yours very truly " or (more friendlier still) " Yours sincerely ". In writing overseas, say to France or U.S.A., it is often courteous to adopt a warmer tone, in keeping with the practice of your correspondent's country.

A less-used alternative to " Yours faithfully " is " Yours truly ". Some firms always use " Yours very truly ". For strictly formal letters neither seems to have an advantage over " Yours faithfully " which is strongly recommended. Such forms as " I am, Sir, Your obedient servant " are considered old-fashioned except in certain official letters. They do not come into normal business correspondence.

There is no need for any alternative to " Yours sincerely ", in most business correspondence. You may sometimes see the rather warmer " Yours very sincerely ", and " Sincerely yours ", particularly in letters from America. In personal correspondence you can follow the salutation " Dear Smith " or " Dear John " with the subscription " Yours ever " or simply " Yours ", but these are really out of place in business letters.

A simple plan is to keep to " Yours faithfully ", " Yours truly ", and " Yours sincerely " for business letters, and let the choice between depend on whether the salutation includes a name, and (as between the last two) whether you are on friendly terms with your correspondent.

Finally comes the signature. If this is not easily legible, the name should be typed or written in capitals underneath, enclosed in brackets. This is a good plan even if the signature is fairly legible.

The signature may be followed by the writer's appointment (" Secretary ", " Director ", etc.) or by such words as " for John Smith & Company Ltd.", according to the practice of the firm.

A woman should always put " Mrs." or " Miss " in brackets after her signature.

To end this chapter a few words will be said about the appearance of a business letter.

The most important thing, of course, is that it should be clear and easy to read. The second thing is that it should be pleasing to the eye.

Both these factors are mainly a matter of layout and design. These words are advertising terms, and in fact most business latters are advertisements—if not actually of goods, then of the firm's services and of the writers themselves. A neat, well-laid-out letter creates an impression of efficiency, and upholds the firm's prestige.

For the same reasons stationery should be good (although not ostentatious or fancy), and envelopes should match the writing paper in quality and colour, and be of such a size that letters do not have to be folded more than twice.

The model below shows a normal framework that can be used for most business letters, whether typed or written by hand.

Phone : EALing 98765

* Ref. : SQ/1234

Park House,
1479 Park Road,
Ealing,
London, W.5.
14*th* August, 19—.

The Secretary,
Messrs. John Smith & Co. Ltd.,
Smith House,
749 Grimsdale Street,
Norwich, Norfolk.

Dear Sir,

Your ref : PST/3567

Thank you for your letter of 12th August.

I have decided to accept your terms, and should like your London representative to call to discuss details. Will you please ask him to make an appointment by phone.

Yours faithfully,

(Henry Brown)

* *or*
HB/MT (*placed here, at foot*)

CHAPTER II

STYLE

THE first rule for all letter-writing is simply this : write as you would speak to your correspondent on that same subject.

Good style is a natural style.

Some writers of business letters seem to think that written English is a different language from spoken English. They avoid the more homely Anglo-Saxon words, such as " ask " and " get " and " buy ", always using the longer French and Latin derived " request " and " acquire " and " purchase ". This can be bad style. There is nothing vulgar about a short word like " buy ", and nothing refined about a longer word like " purchase ".

Suppose that you have ordered a suit of clothes and you want to know when it will be ready. If you call on your tailor, or ring him up, you will probably say something like this :

" Can you tell me when my suit will be ready ? "

Now suppose that you cannot ask him personally, but have to write about it. How would you put the question in a letter ?

Here is one way :

" It would be appreciated if you would advise me when I may expect my suit to become available."

Here is another way :

" Will you please let me know when my suit will be ready."

Which is the better ? The second of course—because it is in the same kind of phraseology as you would use when speaking.

Now let us take the tailor's answer. He is a business man and must write a business-like letter.

Suppose that his answer over the phone would be simply " In about a month ", how would he say this in a letter ?

Here is one way :

" It is anticipated that the article in question will become available within approximately one month from this date."

Here is another way :

" I expect to have your suit ready in about a month's time."

Again the second way is the right way and the first is bad style.

Some business men who use long-winded catch-phrases brush aside criticism of their letters by saying " I'm a business man—I haven't got time for style. I leave that to people who write books. My time's money and I'm not going to waste it on words."

This is a good argument—too good, in fact, for the man making it. If he does not want to waste money on words, he cannot afford to write letters in the bad style that used to be called " business English ". Good style will save him time and, therefore, money.

Compare the examples of good and bad style which have been given here. The first letter to the tailor, which was written in so-called "business English" contains eighteen words. The second letter written in natural English, contains twelve words. The longest word in the second letter is " please "; the first letter contains " appreciated " and " available ".

Now look at the tailor's answer. The letter in " business English " contains eighteen words, including " anticipated ", " available ", and " approximately ". The second letter contains twelve words, of which the longest is " expect ".

These specimens of " business English " are not exaggerated, but are typical of a style of writing that is still fairly widely used. They show that " business English " is bad business as well as bad English.

A business man might argue that he has to be polite, and that he must dress up his words just as he puts out his goods in attractive packages. This is nonsense. There is nothing impolite about using plain words and phrases. A business man would not think twice about using them in business conversation or on the telephone, so why should he bar them from his letters ?

As for wrapping up the words like goods, this argument might be valid if the packages were really attractive. But they are not. " It would be appreciated " is a poor substitute for the good old word " please ", and " become available " sounds pretentious in this case when compared with " be ready ".

A business letter should not only be concise and courteous ; it should also be clear in meaning. If you compare the letters to and from the tailor you will see at once that " business English " is not nearly so clear as ordinary English. The " wrapping up " seems to hide the meaning.

Here is another example of " business English ". It was written by a business man who prided himself that his letters were clear, short, and courteous :

" Yours to hand re packing cases. Delay is regretted, and the matter will be the subject of an immediate investigation on our part."

The writer thought he had done well to say this in twenty-three words. He pointed out proudly that it would have been twenty-four, but he saved a word by leaving out " the " before " delay".

" Translated " into ordinary English, the letter would read ı

" Thank you for your letter about packing cases. We are sorry about the delay, and will look into the matter at once."

Twenty-two words instead of twenty-three ; no long words like " immediate investigation "; no words left out ; and a courteous " Thank you " included—these are the advantages of plain English, because it is plain, is also much clearer in meaning. Moreover, it is just what the business man would have said if he had been talking instead of writing.

" That's all very well," said the business man, when this was pointed out to him, if he had been writing a letter this particular man would probably have said " Your point of view is appreciated,"—" but you can't talk about ' looking into ' things in a letter. That's slang."

It is not slang ; and even slang could be better than the clumsy long-windedness of his " business English ".

Real slang should be avoided in business letters. It serves no purpose and may cause resentment. But slang is a special kind of speech, and must not be confused with ordinary English idioms.

Do not go from one extreme to the other. " We shall proceed immediately " is pointless " business English "; but there is no need to change it to " We shall get on the job right away ". In plain English it is simply, " We shall start work at once".

Many people find it difficult to begin a letter, and a common mistake is starting off on the wrong foot. In letters which are replies to other letters, there is an obvious temptation to begin " In reply to your letter of —— " or " With reference to your enquiry ". The trouble with this sort of beginning is that it is not easy to go on after it. You cannot put a full stop, because you have not yet written a complete sentence ; and if you put a comma after the phrase, which is what it needs, you cannot very well desert it completely and jump at once to packing cases, or whatever you are writing about. The usual way out of the difficulty is to follow such an opening phrase with something like, " we have to inform you that " or " we wish to state that " or " I am writing to confirm that ". This is using a lot of words to say nothing.

The best solution of the problem is to make your

acknowledgement a complete sentence. " Yours to hand " is an example, but a very bad one, because it is certainly not courteous. " We are in receipt of your esteemed favour of the 14th inst." is more polite but very bad style. The way to find the best form of acknowledgement is, as usual, to ask yourself what you would say if you were speaking instead of writing to the person who sent it. This would almost certainly be " Thank you for your letter ". In correspondence you need to put in the date, so it becomes simply, " Thank you for your letter of 14th July ". Having put this down, you can carry on as you wish. You can save yourself all further worries about beginning letters if you adopt this sentence for general use. It is nearly always suitable.

Now let us go back to that sentence, " We are in receipt of your esteemed favour of the 14th inst.", which is an example of " business English " at its worst.

" We are in receipt of " is a clumsy way of saying " We have received "—three words instead of five. " Thank you for " is much better, because it is pleasantly courteous and so makes it unnecessary to refer to the letter as " your esteemed favour ", which is one of the most foolish phrases ever invented.

" Inst." is an abbreviation for the Latin-derived word " instant " used here to mean the current month. " Prox.", meaning next month and " ult." meaning last month, are abbreviations for Latin phrases. All three should be avoided. There is no point in using Latin words in an English letter, and it is much clearer if you name the month. Confusion can easily arise from the old-fashioned inst., ult., and prox. Suppose that you write on 31st August, and ask for delivery of some goods by " 10th prox."—that is, 10th September. Your letter will probably be received on the 1st or 2nd September, and by then 10th September has become " 10th inst." while 10th prox." is now 10th October. Mistakes can easily happen as a result of this. The danger of confusion is avoided entirely if you always use the name of the month instead of any of these three abbreviations.

So by taking the " business English " sentence to pieces, and translating it phrase by phrase, we arrive at the ordinary plain English that is used in good speech as well as in writing. " We are in receipt of your esteemed favour of 14th inst." has become "Thank you for your letter of 14th July," which is shorter, clearer, and more courteous.

More will be said about courtesy later in this chapter. Meanwhile, let us go further into those two other qualities that every business letter should have : brevity and clarity. The two go together, and one rule covers both : say what you mean as simply as you can. Use no more words than are necessary, and choose short words rather than long ones, if they make your meaning as clear.

Do not say " Enclosed please find ": " We enclose " or " I enclose " is shorter and simpler. Do not say " Enclosed herewith ". If an article is enclosed, it must be herewith—and *vice versa*. The two words together are wrong, and bad English. Say either " I am sending herewith " or " I enclose "—the latter is shorter and better.

Avoid all out-moded words such as " hereat ", " therewith ", " hereto " and " thereto ", " hereof " and " thereof ". They are pompous and stilted. You would never use them in conversation, so you cannot need them in letters.

As a general rule, avoid " latter " and " former ", when you should use " this " or " it ". Avoid the word " advise " (except in a term such as " we will advise despatch ") unless you really are giving advice : " I have to advise you " is a bad way of saying " I have to tell you ". Do not say " of even date " for " of to-day ", or " of yesterday's date " for " of yesterday "; and remember that it is always safer and often quicker to write the date in full.

Try not to be flowery. " The favour of your immediate reply will oblige " is a ridiculous way of saying " I shall be glad to hear from you as soon as possible " or " by return ". " Owing to circumstances beyond our control ", can often be replaced by the simpler " through no fault of ours ". Avoid using pointless jargon, and do not be afraid to call a spade a spade. You will not improve your sales by saying " increased consumer resistance has been encountered " when you mean " sales have dropped".

Be careful about the use of the word " position ". Often it is used in mere padding. Do not say " The position regarding the supply of raw materials is deteriorating " when you mean simply, " Raw materials are getting scarcer ". Avoid the constant use of such catch-phrases as " in short supply "; if " scarce " serves your purpose you save two words.

Do not call a " lack " by the mournful-sounding word " dearth " unless you need its full meaning ; and do not say " owing to a lack of timber we are unable to do this " instead of " we cannot do this because we have no timber ", or " because the timber is unobtainable ". " Our stocks of timber are exhausted " is a long-winded way of saying " We have run out of timber ". (The phrase " run out " is idiomatic, but it is not slang).

Other examples of long-windedness are a " considerable period " for a " long time "; " in the near future " for " soon "; " we are of the opinion that " for " we think that "; " we are in agreement " for " we agree"; "we are desirous of" for "we want" or "we should like; " furnish particulars " for " give details "; " owing to unforeseen circumstances " for " unexpectedly"; and " to be of service " for " to serve " or " to help ". There are many others in common use in what is termed " business English ". They are all unbusinesslike.

Watch out for padding, and be ruthless with it. Do not use too many adjectives. Use sparingly the adverb " very ". Do not automatically say a thing is " under active consideration " when you mean only that it is under consideration ; nor should you always speak of a " definite decision ", as if an ordinary decision were vague and indefinite.

Such words as " duly " and such phrases as " it should be pointed out ", " your attention is drawn ", and " kindly note " are usually unnecessary. So are " for your information " " in this connection " and that wretched word " basis " in sentences like, " These goods can be supplied on a sale-or-return basis " which means no more than that " These goods can be supplied on sale or return." Watch the word " case "; " this is not the case " is a weaker way of saying " this is not so ". The word " overall " is often a meaningless variant of " total " and should be avoided. " Involved " is usually a bad word ; why say " This will involve an additional charge of £10 " when you mean " This will cost £10 more ? "

Such phrases as " in relation to ", " in respect of ", " with regard to ", and " in the case of " can nearly always be replaced by the simple words " about " " for ", ' of ", " with ", and " by ".

Even if you are writing on behalf of a firm, there is no need to be too impersonal. Apart from being longer, " it is regretted that " is less courteous than, " I regret " or " we regret ". The same can be said of all these phrases beginning, " it is "—" it is appreciated ", " it is doubtful ", " it is considered ", etc.

Be careful about the word " appreciate ". It does not mean the same as " realize ", although it is often used as if it did. " Aggravate " really means " to make worse "; its use for " to annoy " is colloquial. " Anticipate " is used correctly in the sentence, " The Chancellor of the Exchequer said he could not anticipate his Budget statement "; but the rather simpler word " expect " is often a perfectly good alternative.

The use of the Latin abbreviations " ult." and " prox." has already been mentioned, and all other Latin words should also be avoided. " Per " should not be used for " by "; " as per " may be shorter than " in accordance with ", but if you write plain English instead of " business

English " you can afford to give away a little on the swings for your much bigger gains on the roundabouts ; and " re " is not so good as " about ".

" Approximately " is such a long word that business men often shorten it to " approx." Even this is longer than the plain word " about ". There are many other long words that are common in " business English ". Here is a list of some of them, including several already mentioned in this chapter, with their ordinary alternatives on the right.

The words on the left are not " bad English " in themselves, and most of them have good uses ; but they should not be used when the words on the right will convey the correct meaning.

" BUSINESS ENGLISH " (words to be avoided)	GOOD ENGLISH (words to be used)
acquire	gain, get, win
acquiesce	agree
advise	tell
anticipate	expect
apparent	clear
appreciate	realize
approximately	about
ascertain	find out
assist, assistance	help
available	ready
cease	stop
commence, commencement	begin, beginning
communicate	write
communication	letter
complete (verb)	finish
consider	think
considerable	much
dearth	lack
deem	think
desire	want, wish

dispatch (*verb*)	send
endeavour	try
envisage	expect
expedite	hasten
extend	give
forthwith	at once
grant	give
immediately	at once
implement (*verb*)	carry out
inform	tell
inquire	ask
invariably	always
obtain	get
particulars	details
peruse	read
proceed	go
purchase	buy
request	ask
require, requirement	need
state (*verb*)	say
sufficient	enough
transmit	send
utilise	use

It will be seen that nearly all the words on the right are much shorter than the words on the left.

"Whether", "if" and "though" can on occasion mean the same thing. "It looks as if (*or* as though) he were going to be successful". "See if (*or* whether) you can do it." In these sentences *one* of the meanings of "though" and of "whether" make it correct to use them as alternatives. "If" is often used for "though" however, when it cannot have the right meaning, and it is much better to be correct in such a sentence as : "These articles are in good condition if shop-soiled". There is no avoiding the fact that this sentence really means that the articles must be shop-soiled in order to be in good condition, which is nonsense. What is meant is : "These goods are in good condition, though shop-soiled ". If the words " they are " (which are understood but not necessary in the sentence) are put in before "shop-soiled", it is easy to see why and how, to avoid this error.

Business letters should be courteous ; but courtesy cannot be turned on like water from a tap. Do not end every letter with the same assurance of service and attention, as if the phrase were on a rubber stamp. You merely cheapen courtesy if you write to a man threatening him with legal proceedings unless he pays his debts, and then end your letter by promising him your "best attention at all times ".

Try to make your courtesy personal. Choose the words according to the rest of the letter, and suit the person to whom you are writing.

Do not be servile. Courtesy should at least sound sincere. Similarly, do not beg. " I beg to inform you " and " I beg to state " are meaningless phrases.

CHAPTER III

GRAMMAR AND PUNCTUATION

THERE is no special grammar for business letters—or, indeed, for any kind of letters. English grammar is the same for writing as for speaking. It is not an exact science, and it should be treated as a useful servant rather than a hard master. You cannot write good English, if you are a slave to the rules of grammar—and some of these so-called rules can do more harm than good.

You may have been taught never to end a sentence with a preposition. This is a case in point. " What are these things made of ? " is a simple, decent sentence, and only a person who is afraid of grammar would change it to "Of what are these things made ? " Grammar is not a thing to be afraid of. (The coward would say " Grammar is not a thing of which to be afraid"). The person who keeps turning verbal somersaults in his efforts to stop prepositions from appearing at the ends of sentences will produce the sort of English that once annoyed Mr. Winston Churchill so much that he wrote in the margin of a memorandum, " This is the sort of English up with which I cannot put " !

Another rule that may sometime be broken is the one that says you must not begin a sentence with a conjunction, such as " and " or " but ". It is not a thing to do constantly, but on occasion it may be good and effective.

The thing to remember about grammar is that it is only a convention and not a code of law. It is a useful convention, and should be generally kept ; but it should also be kept in its place, and not allowed to stifle your natural style. Properly used, it will make your letters clear and pleasant to read ; if used badly, it will make them stilted and unnatural.

The so-called " split infinitive " can cause unnecessary trouble. " To consider " is an infinitive : one might call it the name of the verb. If you write " to carefully consider ", the adverb " carefully " has been made to split the infinitive. This is, by purists, held to be bad grammar. As a matter of fact all sensible grammarians agree that there is no reason why you should not split an infinitive sometimes, and that people who make faces or shudder at this " crime " do not know how to use grammar themselves. Still the split infinitive has a bad name, and as it upsets some people it is safest to avoid it. But just occasionally it may be split to avoid artificiality.

The most important rules of grammar are those that help you to make your meaning clear, and if you break these you may cause confusion.

Unattached or wrongly attached participles, for example, may distort the meaning of a sentence. A business firm once wrote to a customer : " We enclose a statement of your account, and being desirous of clearing our books to the end of June, will you please favour us with your cheque in settlement ". The customer wrote back : " You have been misinformed. I have no desire to clear your books to the end of June."

The customer was simply showing what bad grammar had done to the sense of the first letter. The words, " being desirous " were wrongly attached to the word " you ", whereas they were meant to relate to " we ". This mistake could easily have been avoided if the writer had a clear idea of the correct way to use language. If he had put a full stop after " account ", he would probably not have begun the next sentence with a participle at all. Instead, he would have written, " As we are desirous of clearing our books to the end of June, will you please favour us with your cheque in settlement ? " This grammatical English and the meaning is clear, though it would be better if it were put into simpler words, such as : " As we wish to clear our books to the end of June we should be glad if you would settle this account."

Now, even though you have forgotten all you ever learned of grammar, you can avoid grammatical mistakes of this kind if you make sure that your meaning is clear. If you do this, the grammar will often take care of itself.

You might write, " Please tell me if you want these articles ". If you look to see whether you have made your meaning clear, you will quickly see that you have not, because the sentence could mean two different things. It could mean, " Please tell me whether you want these articles " (that is either yes or no) or " If you want these articles, please tell me " (that is either answer yes or do not answer). When you write the sentence you may have the first meaning in your mind, but you cannot complain if the person who gets the letter gives it the second meaning. Then, if he does not want the goods, you will be waiting in vain for an answer.

Correct English is simply clear English. Use words whose meaning you know, and use them in the right place. Think of grammar not as a tyrant but as a friend, without worrying too much about rules.

PUNCTUATION

Punctuation in business letters is simple, if you grasp the way in which it makes the meaning clear. The most commonly used stops are the comma and the full stop.

The Full Stop and Comma

Although it should be an easy matter to decide when to use a comma and when to use a full stop, they are quite often confused in business letters, sometimes making it difficult to understand exactly what is meant. The fault is almost always the same : too many commas and not enough full stops.

It is easy to correct this mistake, if you make a habit of avoiding long and involved sentences. Also it is much easier and quicker to read a letter written in fairly short, direct sentences.

Straightforward, simple sentences need not be abrupt ; and you can use compound, easily flowing sentences without making them too long. If you have a weakness for involved sentences, a good plan is never to begin writing or dictating a sentence until the whole of the sentence is in your mind. There is a limit to the number of words you can keep in your head at once, so if you follow this plan you will force yourself to write only clear sentences. And you will not find yourself floundering in the middle of an involved sentence and wondering how you are going to bring it to an end.

The full stop, full point, or period is used at the end of a set of words that complete a stage of thought. A comma is used to separate words or phrases *within* the sentence that might be wrongly or confusingly run together. Thus if we want to say, " The dog (which chased the cat up the tree) is now indoors " we use commas to separate off the bracketed words. You can judge whether commas are wanted in such a case by considering whether brackets could serve the same purpose, as they do in this example. The reason we do not use brackets is that the comma does the same job without being so obtrusive.

Never use the second comma in such a case without the first once. Commas are also used to separate a series of adjectives and nouns ; " " black, white, red, and green "; " men, women, and children ". Some people, in such cases, omit the comma before " and ", but there is a good case for using it unless " and " separates two words which are closely related.

In modern practice, the comma is *not* used after the number in a street : it is now thought better to write, " 38 Hinsley Road ".

Colon

The colon is used before a following word or words that complete the meaning of the first part of the sentence, where there is no connecting word : " She is obedient : she went without arguing ". Compare this with " She is obedient, so she went without arguing ". The colon construction can be more effective, but it should not be overdone. Because it has this force, the colon is used to introduce a quotation or a number of examples, as in, " We have the following in stock : dictionaries, travel guides, handbooks, children's stories, and novels." (Note that in this last example, without the comma before " and " the meaning might be stories for children and novels).

Semi-colon

This punctuation mark is used to divide parts of a compound sentence that are not sufficiently divided off by a comma. " For young children salads are invaluable because they need the minerals and vitamins for growth ; for adults they provide a means of overcoming the disabilities that accompany civilized ways of life." " This book will be used by the whole family : parents will find help with all kinds of adult entertaining ; children will discover new party games ; everyone will find amusement for quite half an hour." The semi-colon is, like the colon, not very often needed in business correspondence ; but it is useful where it is desired to keep one train of thought running without confusion. Use it before " for " (meaning because) if the reason given is lengthy. If in doubt, break up your matter into clear, shorter sentences.

The Apostrophe before and after S

Some people go through school without ever gaining a clear understanding of the use of the apostrophe for the possessive case of names. If a game is owned by one boy, it becomes " the boy's game " if it belongs to several

boys, it is " the boys' game ". If it is the work belonging
to one day or year, it is " the day's (or year's) work ";
if it goes over several days or years, it is " the days' (or
years') work ". Think of the word you mean (is it " day "
or " days " ?) ; *then* add the apostrophe and s or (after
a plural noun that ends in s) just the apostrophe. After a
singular proper name ending in *s*, add 's : St. James's ;
Miles's ; Marks's ; Jones's.

The Question Mark

The use of the note of interrogation is obvious, but it
is frequently misused at the end of a sentence which
implies a request instead of a question. For example,
" Will you please send me your account ": " Will you
please let me know when I may expect delivery ".
Neither of these phrases requires a question mark at the
end because in each case it is a request or instruction to be
complied with ; not a question. A full stop is the
correct punctuation in such instances because the words
" Will you " are merely included by way of being
courteous.

Paragraphing

You may have been taught that you should begin a new
paragraph when you start a new subject. It is a good
rule, but it needs a little thought. If you were to take it
literally, you could argue that a five-hundred page book
on, for example, electricity, should be written in one
paragraph because it is all about the same subject !

Once again we must remember that this is a device to
help somebody else to take in our meaning easily. The
end of a sentence gives a mental " breathing-space ", and
the end of a paragraph gives a longer one. These are the
steps by which your argument is built up by you and taken
in by your correspondent.

In business letters it is particularly important to ensure
that no point is overlooked. Short paragraphs will help.
If you are writing about three separate orders, each can be

dealt with in a separate paragraph. But if there is a great deal to be said about each order, this again may be broken down into several paragraphs, each dealing with one *aspect* of the order. Sentences grouped into one paragraph should all be related to the same subject; but it sometimes occurs that one sentence alone makes a paragraph, because it is not closely related to what comes before and after it. Many people who dictate letters train themselves to say " paragraph " at the right places ; but if this is not done the shorthand-typist should mark her paragraphs when reading through her notes before typing.

CHAPTER IV

METHOD

WHETHER your business correspondence is much or little, it will pay you to deal with it methodically. Method is a time-saver—and " time is money ".

Your first task is to train yourself to answer letters promptly. Very few persons actually like writing business letters, and it is a human tendency to delay doing unpleasant things as long as possible. This tendency must be overcome ; and it is a fact that the less you delay, the less unpleasant letter-writing becomes. If you answer letters promptly it saves you the trouble of making excuses to yourself for not answering them. " I haven't the time—I'm too busy " is the usual excuse. The less time you have, and the busier you are, the less you can afford to allow your letters to pile up.

It is a matter of self-discipline, and the method to be employed depends upon your circumstances. You may find it necessary to set aside a fixed time of the day for answering letters. If you do, keep to it. The best plan is to make it a rule to answer all letters by return of post. Promptness is appreciated in business and a reputation for quick replies is a good business asset. It suggests efficiency.

There may be some exceptions to the return-of-post rule. Sometimes you may have to write an important letter on which much will depend. It may be a reply to a letter that calls for difficult decisions or a definite policy that will have far-reaching effects on your business. You may want to think the matter over—perhaps sleep on it, or consult others. It is wise to do so. Promptness does not mean haste, and thinking before you write is never a waste of time. But do not use this as an excuse from running away from a letter that is difficult to write. Once you have decided what you want to say there is no justification for further delay.

Delay may be advisable also when you are annoyed. An angry business letter rarely does good and often does harm, and a rude letter is always a mistake.

The second important matter is accuracy, and this begins when you read letters addressed to yourself. It is astonishing how many people in business are inaccurate readers.

Read carefully each letter which you receive, and keep your thoughts on what you are reading. Remember that the person who wrote it probably has a different style from yours in expressing himself ; and make sure that you really understand what he means.

Read each letter again just before you reply to it, and keep it in front of you when you are making your reply. Do not rely on your memory even for a short time, or you may overlook some point needing your comment.

As has been shown in the previous chapter, the object of a letter is to communicate your thoughts to another person ; and therefore your own letters should be precise as well as clear. Take into account the possibility that the person you are writing to may be a careless reader, and make it your aim to give him or her no chance of misunderstanding you. If your letter is misunderstood, you may be able to tell yourself that it was not your fault and that the other person is a fool ; but this is no consolation if the result is extra work for you or perhaps even loss of business. Your letter may have been clear enough to you and to your secretary, but that is not the point : the question you must ask yourself is whether it could have been even clearer.

Unless a letter is a simple acknowledgement of a very short request or reply, it is advisable to jot down notes of what you want to say before you start. Each point in your notes will probably be a paragraph in the letter. Indeed, if you do this beforehand you will not have to think about paragraphing—it will come automatically.

If you have to answer a number of questions, deal with them one by one, in the order given. Do not try to answer two questions with one sentence, and do not go back to a question once you have answered it.

If you yourself are asking questions, separate them in the same way. Similarly, if you are giving information, split it up into a number of facts.

The foregoing remarks apply equally whether you write or type your letters yourself or whether you dictate them to a stenographer. There are, however, certain additional points that need to be remembered in dictating.

In the first place, short sentences are most desirable. It has been said that there is a limit to the length of sentence that one can hold in one's mind at a time ; and you *must* have the whole sentence in your mind before you start dictating it. It is no good beginning the sentence with only a vague idea of how it will continue, and just hoping that it will work out all right in the end. Think of the sentence first ; then say it, and do not continue dictating until the whole of the next sentence is already in your mind.

Incidentally, dictating letters is a great improver of style in letter-writing. It forces you to use short, clear sentences. If you find it difficult to dictate, it is probably because your normal style is bad. It will remain bad if you refuse to dictate, and it is futile to try to convince yourself that the difficulty has any other reason. Dictating is a valuable exercise for the letter-writer, and the person who finds it hardest needs it the most.

Another useful effect of dictating is that it makes your style more natural and less pompous. The very fact that you are speaking instead of writing makes you more likely to use English as it is spoken and not the peculiar artificial written language described in an earlier chapter. You would not talk to your secretary (if you have one) about " commencing " or " endeavouring " or " envisaging ", and the fact that you speak the letter to her may influence you to use more sensible words like " beginning " and " trying " and " expecting ".

When dictating, how far you can leave the punctuation to your stenographer depends on her. If she is sufficiently intelligent, you can merely indicate the stops by pauses. But you must pause in the right places, and it is unreasonable to expect her to transform a badly dictated letter into a piece of good English prose. As you go along, you should tell her when you want such things as inverted commas (quotes) and capital letters used, unless these are obvious ; and it is a good plan to say when you want a new paragraph to begin.

Dictating letters through the medium of a Dictaphone, or other recording instrument, has its advantages. You can use it in your own time ; there is no danger of mistakes being made by a stenographer in " reading back " her shorthand ; and most important of all, you can " play back " the record to yourself and so judge whether the letter is good.

Everyone who uses such an instrument should " play back " regularly, if only to see whether the dictation was really clear. The first time you use one of these dictating machines, you will probably be horrified to hear how badly you dictated—especially in the use of pauses to indicate punctuation marks.

Reading through and signing letters may not seem to call for much method, but these are very important matters. Most people find reading their own letters a tedious job, and are tempted to skim through them very quickly. There is an oft quoted case of a secretary with a sense of humour who one day typed into a letter the sentence, " I never read letters before I sign them "— and then pointed it out to her chief *after* he had signed !

There are two good reasons why you should read every letter carefully before signing it. One is that your typist is human ; the other is that you are human—and human beings make mistakes.   If you have written or typed the letter yourself, mistakes are still possible.

If your typist is well trained and conscientious, she will have read the letter herself to correct any typing errors. But she will not have corrected mistakes in her shorthand, unless such errors became obvious to her upon reading through her notes or transcriptions.   These mistakes may be due to her faulty shorthand-writing or " reading back "; but they may be due to your slovenly pronunciation.

Then there are the mistakes that you may have made, and which you did not realize, when you were dictating the letter.   You see them when your words stare up at you from the paper—and you wonder how you could have made such a slip or expressed yourself so badly.

You may find also that you no longer feel so sure that you have said the right things.   When you were pacing up and down the office floor, flinging words at your secretary, you may have said things that sounded pretty good, but which do not look nearly so satisfactory when they are down in black and white.   Perhaps you made a joke which was only funny when your tone of voice could be heard and which may be taken as an insult when read in a letter.   Perhaps you used words that, when pleasantly spoken, were agreeable enough, but which might seem curt and rude when transmitted by the impersonal typewriter.   And perhaps you have second thoughts after " getting it off your chest ".

Whenever anything like this happens, the only sensible course is to start the letter afresh.   Do not, for the sake of saving time or money, send the letter as it is despite your misgivings.   You will probably regret it the moment it has been posted—and if you think there is a chance that it may be unfavourably received, it is almost certain that it will be.   The business man who makes mistakes is not doomed to failure on that account ; but his chances of success are greatly reduced if he will not admit and correct mistakes when he has the chance.

Having read the letter and satisfied yourself that it conveys what you want to say, sign it and check the enclosures if there are any, unless you can trust your typist to do this. Remember that sending letters without enclosures is quite a common fault in offices.

A carbon copy should be kept of every outgoing letter, and the usual practice is to clip together all letters on the same subject. Copies of letters requiring answers should be kept in a separate tray or folder; others should be filed and indexed in such a way that they can be found quickly a long time afterwards.

There are many different filing systems, but no general rules are of much help. Each office has its own special needs, and the best plan is to devise or adapt the system most suited to your purpose.

PART II

MODEL BUSINESS LETTERS

ONLY the "body" of each letter is given, as the framework is similar for all. For details of the framework see Chapter I.

CHAPTER V

EMPLOYMENT

1. *Applying for a Job*

Dear Sir,

I wish to offer my services for the post of Sales Manager which you advertised as vacant in to-day's *Daily Telegraph*.

I enclose a short summary of my qualifications and experience, together with copies of three recent testimonials.

Should you consider me a suitable applicant, I would suggest a commencing salary of £—— a year, and should be pleased to call for an interview at any time convenient to you.

Yours faithfully,

2. *Applying for a Job*

Dear Sir,

I wish to apply for the post of shorthand-typist which you advertised as vacant in to-day's *Daily Telegraph*.

I am eighteen years of age.   I was educated at ———— School, gained the Certificate of ————, and have just finished a commercial course at ———— College. My shorthand speed is ———— words a minute, and my typing speed ———— words a minute.

Yours faithfully,

3. *From an Employer, offering an Interview*

Dear Sir,

Thank you for your letter of 10th January.

Will you please call to see me on Tuesday, 18th January, at 10.30 a.m.

If you cannot call at this time, perhaps you will phone my secretary for another appointment.

Yours faithfully,

4. *Reply to the previous letter*

Dear Sir,

Thank you for your letter of 12th January.

I shall be pleased to call at your office on Tuesday, 18th January, at 10.30 a.m.

Yours faithfully,

5. *From an Applicant, postponing an interview*

Dear Sir,

Thank you for your letter of 20th August.

I am sorry to say I cannot come to see you on Wednesday, 28th August, as you suggested, but I could call at any time on any other day next week.

Will you kindly give me another appointment.

Yours faithfully,

6. *From a former Employee, asking for a Reference*

Dear Mr. Smith,

When I left the office, you kindly said you would give me a reference if I needed one.

I have now been offered the sort of job I want, subject to my producing a satisfactory reference, and should be very grateful if you would give me one.

I hope that you are keeping well,

Yours sincerely,

7. *Reply to Previous Letter*

Dear Jones,

I was very pleased to hear your good news, and I enclose a reference. I mean every word of it, so you can ask your future employer to get in touch with me if he wants to know any more about you.

I am keeping pretty fit, and things are much the same here as they were when you left. We shall always be pleased to see you if you have time to call.

Wishing you the best of luck in your new job,

Yours sincerely,

8. *From a Prospective Employer to a Former Employer*

Confidential

Dear Sir,

Mr. John Smith, of 84 Park Road, Boxton, has applied for a position with us as Sales Manager, and he has said that he used to work for you.

I should be glad if you would give me, in confidence, your opinion of Mr. Smith's ability and character, and also details of the kind of work he did when he was with you.

Yours faithfully,

9. *Reply to the Previous Letter* (1)

<u>Confidential</u>

Dear Sir,

Thank you for your letter of 12th October.

Mr. John Smith worked here from —— to ——, and for the last twelve months he was our Sales Manager.   As I expect he told you, he left because he had to move south owing to his wife's ill-health.   We were sorry to lose him, and I can confidently recommend him for a similar post.

Mr. Smith is energetic, hard-working and entirely trustworthy.   He has plenty of initiative, and knows how to handle staff.

Yours faithfully,

10. *Reply to No. 8 Letter* (2)

<u>Confidential</u>

Dear Sir,

Thank you for your letter of 12th October.

Mr. John Smith worked here from —— to ——, and for the last three months he was our Sales Manager.   We found him entirely honest and trustworthy, but I am bound to tell you that we were forced to end his engagement with us owing to repeated divergence of opinions between him and his superiors.   I must therefore confine my reference to his character, which was beyond reproach.

Yours faithfully,

11. *From an Employee, asking for a Rise*

Dear Mr. Smith,

I wish to ask for an increase in my salary.

This has been unchanged for three years, although new responsibilities have been added to my work.

As I think you know, I am happy in my job, and I have no wish to look for anything else. But I have fresh expenses at home now that my two children are growing up, and I am finding it hard to live on my present income.

I should be grateful if you would consider this request.

Yours very truly,

12. *From an Employee, explaining Absence from Work*

Dear Mr. Smith,

I am sorry that I have not been able to come to the office this week. As my wife told you over the phone, I went down with 'flu last Sunday, and have had to spend three days in bed.

The doctor came again this morning, and said that I could get up for a few hours, but he did not think I would be fit to return to work for another week.

I am sorry to have caused you trouble in this way, and 1 hope I shall soon be able to get back to the office.

My Doctor's certificate is enclosed.

Yours sincerely,

13. *Reply to the Previous Letter*

Dear Jones,

I was sorry to hear that you were laid up, and I hope you are feeling better now. We are managing to cope with your work fairly well in your absence, so do not come back until you are really fit again.

Best wishes.

Yours sincerely,

14.   *From a Parent, explaining Absence from Work*

Dear Sir,

I am sorry to have to tell you that my daughter Mary will not be able to come to work this week, as she is suffering from 'flu.

The doctor cannot say yet when Mary will be fit again, but she will write to you herself as soon as she is allowed out of bed.   She asks me to say that she is very sorry for any inconvenience her absence may cause you.

I enclose the doctor's certificate.

Yours faithfully,

15.   *Reply to the Previous Letter*

Dear Mrs. Jones,

I was very sorry to hear of your daughter's illness, and I hope she will soon be better again.

Please tell Miss Jones not to worry about the office.   I am sure you will not let her return to work until she is fit for it, and of course we do not want her to come until she feels herself again.

Thank you for the medical certificate.

Yours sincerely,

16.   *From a Traveller, sending in Orders*

Dear Mr. Smith,

I enclose the orders obtained in this town.   You will see that they include two new customers, both of whom may do quite a lot of business with us.

I am leaving to-morrow for Dockton, where I shall be staying at the Station Hotel.   I expect to be there for about a week.

Yours sincerely,

17. *From a Traveller, offering his Services*

Dear Sirs,

I am travelling for Messrs. ——— in ——— and for Messrs. ——— in ———, and I can take on another line that does not compete with either of these.

My territory covers most of the Midlands, and I have a very good connection with the large stores in Birmingham.

I should like to carry your goods, because I feel sure I could sell them. If you are willing to give me the chance will you please tell me your terms ?

I expect to be in London towards the end of next month, and will gladly call on you if you wish.

Yours faithfully,

CHAPTER VI

DEBTOR AND CREDITOR

18. *Asking for an Account to be rendered*

Dear Sirs,

Will you please send me a detailed statement of your account up to 30th June.

Yours faithfully,

19. *Reply to the Previous Letter*

Dear Sir,

Thank you for your letter of 5th July.

We enclose our detailed account up to 30th June, as requested.

Yours faithfully,

20. *Disputing an Account*

Dear Sirs,

Thank you for your letter of 8th July and your account. Two items seem to be incorrect.

Item No. 3 (£42 10s.) does not agree with your quotation of 5th April (£38 15s.)

You have not credited me with the value of goods returned on 25th June (£8 12s.), for which I hold your carrier's receipt.

If you will amend the account, I will send you a cheque in settlement.

Yours faithfully,

21. *Reply to the Previous Letter*

Dear Sir,

Thank you for your letter of 10th July.

We greatly regret that we failed to credit you with £8 12s. for the goods returned on 25th June. We enclose amended account.

In answer to your query about item No. 3 (£42 10s.) we would remind you that our quotation of 5th April was given on the understanding that any increase in price before delivery would have to be added. You accepted this condition when you placed your order.

We trust you will agree that our account is now in order.

Yours faithfully,

22. *From a Creditor to a Debtor, demanding Payment* (*Mild*)

A statement of our account was sent to you on the 31st August.

In case you did not receive this, we enclose a copy and should be grateful if you would let us have your remittance in settlement.

Yours faithfully,

23. *From a Creditor to a Debtor, demanding Payment* (*Stronger*)

Dear Sir,

We would remind you that our account for August is still outstanding.

As this is long overdue, we must ask you to let us have settlement at an early date.

Yours faithfully,

24. *From a Creditor to a Debtor, demanding Payment (Very Strong)*

Dear Sir,

Unless our account is settled within seven days, we shall have to place the matter in the hands of our solicitors.

Yours faithfully,

25. *From a Debtor to a Creditor, asking for Time*

Dear Sirs,

I am very sorry about the delay in payment of my account. I know it is overdue, and I am grateful for the patience you have already shown.

Unfortunately I am still unable to settle this account, as I in turn am awaiting payments due to me. My debtors, however, have promised settlement within the next two weeks, and if you will give me a similar period of grace I shall be able to clear your account.

I regret having to ask you this, but would remind you that I have always been able to pay promptly in the past. I feel sure I shall be able to do so in the future, too.

Yours faithfully,

26. *To a Bank Manager, asking him to stop payment of a Cheque*

Dear Sir,

Will you please stop the payment of cheque No. XBM 1756486 dated 10th March, for £100, drawn in favour of John Smith.

Yours faithfully,

CHAPTER VII

WHOLESALE AND RETAIL

In the model letters given in this chapter, the Supplier may be a Manufacturer or Wholesale Factor, and the Distributor may be a Wholesale Factor or a Retailer, dependent upon the class of trade to which the examples are applied.

27. *From a Supplier to a Distributor, seeking Custom*

Dear Sir,

We have pleasure in enclosing our latest catalogue, which we think will be of interest to you.

Our terms are ————.

We shall be pleased to send you any samples you may want, and our representative will call at your request.

Yours faithfully,

28. *From a Distributor to a Supplier, asking for Information*

Dear Sirs,

Will you please send me your catalogue of lawn mowers, and also let me know your terms.

At the same time perhaps you will tell me how soon I might expect delivery after placing an order.

Yours faithfully,

29. *Reply to the Previous Letter*

Dear Sir,

Thank you for your letter of 1st August.

We have pleasure in enclosing our catalogue of lawn mowers.

Our terms are ———.

Deliveries are normally made within three weeks of receipt of orders. However, this does not apply at present to our model No. LX 424 (page 33 of the catalogue) for which the delivery period is two months. We shall reduce both these periods as soon as we can.

Our representative will be pleased to call on you at your request.

Yours faithfully,

30. *From a Supplier to a Distributor, asking for a Reference*

Dear Sir,

Thank you for your letter of 10th August.

Before opening an account with you, we would ask you to provide a reference.

This is, of course, an ordinary routine request, before the opening of any new credit account.

Yours faithfully,

31. *Reply to the Previous Letter*

Dear Sirs,

Thank you for your letter of 12th August.

My reference is my local bank. The address is :

Yours faithfully,

32. *From a Supplier, taking up a Commercial Reference*

Confidential

Dear Sir,

Mr. ——— of ——— wishes to open an account with us, and has given us your name as a reference.

Would you kindly let us know, in confidence, whether you consider Mr. ———'s financial position justifies our allowing him credit for, say £100.

Yours faithfully,

33. *Reply to the Previous Letter*

Confidential

Dear Sir,

In reply to your letter of 14th August, we are able to state that Mr. ——— of ——— has had an account with us for ——— years, and, to the best of our knowledge, his financial position is sound.

Judging from our business dealings with Mr. ———, there should be no risk attached to your allowing him credit for £100.

Yours faithfully,

34. *Alternative Reply to No. 32 Letter*

Confidential

Dear Sir,

In reply to your letter of 14th August, we regret that we cannot recommend your allowing Mr. ——— of ——— credit beyond £50.

Yours faithfully,

35. *From a Supplier to a Distributor giving limited Credit*

Dear Sir,

Thank you for your letter of 13th August.

We are pleased to inform you that we are willing to open an account with you, and to allow you credit up to £100, with terms of 25% discount, settlement monthly.

You may be assured of our prompt attention to your orders.

Yours faithfully,

36. *From a Supplier to a Distributor, refusing Credit*

Dear Sir,

Thank you for your letter of 13th August.

We regret that, at present, we are unable to open a credit account with you, but we shall be pleased to meet your requirements on receipt of cash with order.

Yours faithfully,

37. *From a Distributor to a Supplier, complaining about Goods*

Dear Sirs,

I received to-day the consignment of lawn mowers referred to in your Advice Note No. 132 of 28th March.

I ordered six machines Model LX 424, but only four were included in the consignment. Will you please let me know whether the other two are being sent separately and, if so, when I may expect them.

Yours faithfully,

38. *Reply to the Previous Letter*

Dear Sir,

Thank you for your letter of 31st March.

We regret that we were only able to send four of the machines Model LX 424 in this consignment, as a result of an unforeseen hold-up in production.

It is expected that the other two machines will be ready within about ten days, and a further Advice Note will be sent you at time of dispatch.

We are very sorry if this delay has caused you any inconvenience.

Yours faithfully,

39. *From a Distributor to a Supplier, demanding Delivery*

Dear Sirs,

On 25th February I ordered twelve lawn mowers Model 424 on the understanding that these would be delivered within two months.

These machines are now a fortnight overdue, and I need them urgently. Will you please let me know when I may expect them.

Yours faithfully,

40. *From a Distributor to a Supplier, demanding Delivery (stronger)*

Dear Sirs,

On 12th February I ordered twelve lawn mowers Model 424 on the understanding that these would be delivered within two months.

These machines are now a month overdue, and the delay is serious for me. As you know, the demand for these goods is seasonal, so unless I can get immediate delivery I shall be forced to cancel the order and buy from another firm.

Yours faithfully,

41. *Reply to the two Previous Letters*

Dear Sir,

Thank you for your letter of 13th May.

We greatly regret the delay in delivering the lawn mowers, and would assure you that it is due to circumstances outside our control.

However, we are pleased to inform you that the goods are now almost ready for despatch, and we can promise delivery within the next seven days.

Please accept our sincere apologies for any inconvenience which this delay may mean to you.

Yours faithfully,

CHAPTER VIII

MISCELLANEOUS

42. *From a Customer to a Manufacturer, asking for Service*

Dear Sirs,

Will you please arrange for your representative to call and inspect my washing machine, which has stopped working.

I bought this washing machine on 10th August last. The guarantee number is XQ 27468.

Yours faithfully,

43. *From a Customer to a Manufacturer, returning Goods*

Dear Sirs,

I enclose my electric shaver, which I bought on 10th August last, under the terms of my guarantee No. XQ 27468.

During the last two weeks the shaver has been working erratically, and I think it needs attention. I have tried it from two different supply points and the fault is definitely not in the current.

Yours faithfully,

44. *From a Retailer to Customers (Circular Letter)*

Dear Madam,

Have you seen our new display of soft furnishings?

We think we are offering some exceptional bargains, and the sales so far indicate that our opinion is shared by many of our customers.

Our stocks are limited, and we regret that it is unlikely that we shall be able to repeat these offers. If you are thinking of buying any soft furnishings, or if you are likely to need any in the near future, we earnestly recommend you to inspect our range now.

The enclosed leaflet gives details of some of our bargains.

Any order with which you may favour us will receive our prompt and careful attention.

Yours faithfully,

45. *From a New Retailer to old Customers* (*Circular Letter*)

Dear Madam,

I expect you know that Mr. ——— has decided to sell his business, and I am writing to introduce myself as his successor. I shall be taking over on 15th August.

I shall esteem the continuation of the patronage that you have given to Mr. ———, and I shall do my best to carry out your orders promptly and efficiently.

While the general running of the business will be unchanged, I intend to make a few innovations which I am sure will improve the service, and meet with your approval.

Yours faithfully,

46. *From a New Retailer seeking New Customers* (*Circular Letter*)

Dear Madam,

I am writing to tell you that this business is now under entirely new ownership and management.

I intend to make many innovations in order to improve the service, and some of these are already being put into effect. I hope you will give me the chance of earning your patronage.

Yours faithfully,

47. *From a Business man apologizing for Absence*

Dear Mr. Smith,

I am sorry to have to tell you that I shall be unable to attend the meeting on Tuesday, 4th September, for personal reasons.

Will you please convey my regrets to all concerned.

Yours sincerely,

48. *From a Business man postponing an Interview*

Dear Mr. Smith,

I am sorry to have to tell you that, owing to unforeseen circumstances, I shall be unable to come up to London on Tuesday, 4th September.

Could we make another appointment ? I shall be able to come any day during the week 10th to 15th September.

Yours sincerely,

49. *From a Customer to a Newsagent, suspending delivery*

Dear Sir,

Will you please discontinue delivery of papers for a fortnight from next Sunday—that is, from 3rd July to 16th July inclusive.

We shall require the papers again as usual from 17th July.

Yours faithfully,

50. *From a Householder to a Builder*

Dear Sir,

I have a number of small jobs that need doing, including replacement of tiles and repairs to the garage doors.

Will you please come and look at the repairs needed and give me an estimate. Perhaps you will phone to let me know when you can call.

Yours faithfully,

51. *From a Tenant to a Landlord regarding Repairs*

Dear Sir,

I should be grateful if you would give your attention to the roof at these premises. It is in urgent need of repair.

As a result of last night's storm, water has dripped through into two of the bedrooms, and there are wet patches on the wall of the hall.

Yours faithfully,

52. *From a Landlord to a Tenant, raising the Rent*

Dear Sir,

I am writing to tell you that I am compelled to increase your rent from —— per month to —— per month.

Being on an inclusive rental, you will realise that this is due to the increased rates which I have to pay. The net rent which I shall receive will be unchanged.

The increase will date from 1st August, when the next payment is due.

Yours faithfully,

53. *From a Tenant to a Landlord, regarding the Rent*

Dear Sir,

I regret to have to ask you to allow me to defer payment of my rent for a short period.

I am very sorry to have to make this request, but I am in temporary financial difficulty. I have been away from work owing to illness for nearly six weeks, and the insurance benefits have not been enough to keep my family. I have already used up my savings.

I am back at work now, and I am confident that I shall soon be financially sound again. If you will give me a month's grace I hope to be able to clear off the arrears very shortly.

Yours faithfully,

54 *From a Tenant to a Landlord, giving Notice*

Dear Sir,

In accordance with the terms of our agreement, I am writing to give you one month's notice that I shall vacate these premises on 30th September next.

Yours faithfully,